HEARTBREAK
to HEALING
Reclaiming Your Life
After the Loss of a Spouse

Amanda Banks

Dedication

I dedicate this book to my first love, who I will always hold deep in my heart. Your strength showed me how to become strong within myself. Your life touched my soul and together we created a family that can never be broken by the bonds of death.

Introduction

Losing a spouse and learning to move on with your life can be very difficult. While you may often hear that time heals all wounds, the truth is, some wounds cannot be healed with time. It is normal to feel as though a part of you is missing when your spouse is taken from you, and dealing with the grief surrounding that loss can be enormous.

Each person has a different story and different ways to handle their situation. My experience started out as a beautiful love story. My husband and I were childhood sweethearts. We dated all through high school, and got married in our early twenties. We were blessed with two beautiful daughters within the first five years of being married. Then the unspeakable happened. He became very sick, and passed away within two years of diagnosis. Explaining all of this to my children and trying to help them cope with the loss of their father has been tough. Trying to heal from my own loss and grief, while staying strong for my daughters has been a challenge, but we have adapted and have begun to live again.

If you have lost your spouse, there are many things that you must do to move on with your life. One of the most important, is dealing with the grief that is surrounding your loss. With this book, you will learn the many steps that you can go through to help you move on past your loss and begin to heal and live life once more. These steps have helped my family and I hope that they can help yours as well.

Amanda Banks

Chapter 1 - What is Grief?

Grief is defined as a "keen mental suffering or distress over affliction or loss; sharp sorrow; painful regret." However, it is actually a lot more than just that. In fact, there are many stages that one must go through to deal with grief.

Depression is normal throughout this process and you should not force yourself to move on until you are ready. It is even likely that you will feel depression and sadness eight months or more after the event occurred. You are likely to find others who do not understand your grief. These are the people who tell you that you just need to get over it and move on with your life. Just remember that everything that you are feeling is normal, and it is okay to want to be alone during the time that you are healing.

Below, you will find more information regarding the different stages you will most likely experience:

Denial
The first thing that most people say when they lose someone close to them is that they feel numb. It is

most likely that you will even feel denial that the death occurred, which is usually a way that your body chooses to avoid feeling the pain that goes along with your loss. Most people also go into some form of shock and this helps provide protection from the emotions that can be overwhelming if felt all at one time. This first stage can last for weeks.

In my case, I was in denial when my husband was diagnosed with his illness. I just couldn't come to terms with the facts that he was terminal, and that my kids and I would soon be alone. This is a common coping mechanism our brains provide to help us cope with stress.

Guilt

When your shock does finally begin to wear off, it is likely to be replaced with extreme pain that is excruciating. While this pain may seem unbearable, you should not try and hide from your pain. Instead, feel it fully and above all do not resort to trying to mask your pain with drugs and alcohol. If you find yourself in this situation, you should seek help immediately. During this stage, it is also common for you to feel remorse over the things that you did or did not do with your spouse. This is also completely normal, but life will feel scary during this phase as well and at times chaotic.

When my husband was sick, I felt guilty for being healthy. I wanted to take away his pain, but I couldn't. Even now, many years later, I will feel a pang of guilt, wondering if there was anything else I could have done to save him. I know in my heart that there was nothing that could be done, but guilt has a way of taking over at times when we are feeling weak. We just need to be able to recognize that is is unrealistic and try to focus on taking care of ourselves.

Anger

When you reach this phase of the grieving process, you may begin lashing out at others around you and begin blaming them for the one that you have lost. While this is the time to let all your emotions out into the open, you should try to control how you react to others. If you are not careful, you risk causing damage to the relationships of the people you have around you. Instead of yelling at others, sit in your car with the windows rolled up and scream and cry as loud as you can, or punch a pillow with all of your might. Get it out or it will fester and become out of control.

Be patient with your children during this time. They are also trying to process the experience and do not have the coping tools that we, as adults have developed.

Depression

This is usually the stage where people begin to think that you should be moving on with your life. However, this is also the time that you may begin experiencing a long period of sadness where you spend much of your time reflecting about the past. Just remember that this is a part of the grieving process, and you should not feel bad that you are still sad about your loss. Emptiness and despair are also feelings that typically go along with this stage as well.

If you find that you are not taking good care of yourself by not showering, not eating and sleeping all day, you could be suffering from major depression, and you should seek professional help.

Acceptance and Hope

Eventually, you will begin to feel that your life is adjusting and you are beginning to return to normal. During this time, you may feel as if your depression and sadness lifts some. During this final stage, your mind will begin to focus on other things besides your loss, and you will begin rebuilding your life without your spouse. Finally, you will begin to accept what has happened.

After you have gone through the stages of grief, you should keep in mind that although you have accepted the situation, this does not mean that you are happy again. There is a good and likely chance that you will never return to the person who you were before you lost your spouse. Losing someone this close to you is a traumatic experience and just because the pain and sadness may have subsided, you may have lasting effects from losing your loved one. Rest assured, however, that you can find happiness once more and finally begin living a life that is fresh and new.

You CAN get through this!

Chapter 2 - Grieving with Others

When you lose someone as close as a spouse, it is common for those who love you to draw closer to you in your time of need. This can be extremely comforting, but there are times when you wish to be with yourself. You should keep in mind that the others in your life are going through some of the same process that you are, and are looking to express their grief in helping you out in any way that they can. Sometimes, this outpouring of love can be overwhelming, and it is natural to pull inward at times.

If you do find yourself confronted with some of these situations, try to be honest with people rather than allowing them to continue being around constantly. You should start by graciously thanking them for their love and support during the time that you need it the most. Then explain to them that even though you definitely value and need their support that you will also want to spend some time for yourself as well. Assure them that when you do need them that you will call.

You should also make sure that you do call these

people when you need them. Don't feel as though you are alone in the situation. There are always people around that love you and will support you. When you are feeling down and need a shoulder to cry on or need some groceries, but are not feeling up to venturing outside of your home, rely on these people who offered their assistance. It can be a blessing to have them around when you need them.

After you have gone through the stages of grief that you are most likely going to be passing through, be sure to thank these people for all of the help that they provided you during your time of need. Have them over for dinner in order to show your appreciation for everything that they did for you during your healing process.

After my husband passed away, all I wanted to do was be alone. That is just my personality. I don't like a lot of people around me when I am upset. It is okay to want to be alone, and we need that peace and quiet to absorb what we have gone through, and to mentally process and adjust to our new life. As long as you are not shutting out the world entirely, alone time is beneficial, and you don't need to feel guilty or ashamed for needing to take this time for yourself and your family.

Chapter 3 - Making Arrangements

Immediately following the death of your spouse, just when your life is being uprooted and thrown into a whirlwind, you will suddenly find yourself in a situation where you are expected to complete the impossible; plan the funeral for your spouse. This is probably going to be one of the hardest things to handle at this point in the process. If you have older children or close loved ones, this is one of the best times to rely on them for support and guidance.

There are many things that you must do during this time. With the support of others, you will be able to get through this time and begin the difficult path of healing that lay before you. If possible, it is easiest if you plan the following items before the death occurs. Planning ahead for the unthinkable may be difficult, but it can make the process go much smoother and help give you the time that you need to grieve properly without the stress of planning a funeral.

Below are some of the items that you will need to make sure you take care of in the few weeks following the death of your spouse:

Call the local funeral home

If you have any plans that you have made with your spouse beforehand, be sure you bring them with you. Likewise, you will want to bring and deeds to grave plats, pre-paid cremation documentation or any discharge papers from the military if your spouse has any. You will also need to bring any instructions that were left behind by your spouse in regards to any viewing and burial preferences. You should also keep in mind that it is common for friends and family members to contact the funeral home in order to learn more about the arrangements, like the date and time of the services that will be taking place. You will need to leave any instructions, such as flower arrangement or donation requests with the funeral home so that they can relay this to the guests who wish to pay their respect.

Write an Obituary

This will be difficult to do, so it is a good idea to have family around for support during this process. You should include your spouse's education, career, any military service that they may have had, surviving family and anything else that would help showcase their life to those attending the funeral. This information will help the funeral director when providing obituaries for the local newspapers.

Obtain Certified Death Certificates

You will need these documents for many things, such as closing IRA's and dealing with outstanding loans and bank accounts. You should request about 10 certified copies and keep one on file for future use. These can usually be requested from the funeral director or a country office. If you are unsure of the procedure, your funeral director will be able to guide you in the right direction. They usually cost about $12 each, so be prepared to pay over $100 for the copies that you need to order.

Review Will or Trust Documents

Since it is your spouse that passed, everything will most likely return to you. However, if there is a will to consider you will need to remove it from safe keeping at this time. These documents will need to be filed with the Probate Court where you and your spouse are residents. However, you should first take the documents to your attorney and allow them to file the paperwork for you.

Consult with your Attorney

When you deliver the will to your attorney, you should also review the situation with them at this time. It is difficult to say whether you will need your attorney or not for the probate or trust administration, so it is best that you discuss with them the next steps that you need to take. It is extremely important that wills are handled carefully and filed properly in order to avoid any legal liability that may come from the mishandling of the paperwork.

Contact Current and Former Employers

From current and former employers, you will need to obtain the information regarding life insurance and any other benefits that may be awarded to you. It is best to have them mail or fax a statement of benefits for your spouse so that you will know exactly the items that you will need to handle in order to get the most from the benefits that your spouse was being offered.

Contact Social Security Offices

The Social Security Administration will need to be contacted regarding the death of your spouse. If they were drawing their social security or entitled to it, you may be able to receive a death benefit from it. There are some requirements about the length of the marriage, but they will be able to help walk you through the process.

Life Insurance and Annuity

You will also need to gather the information required by the insurance company in order to receive the settlement for the life insurance policy. In order to do this, you will need to process a claim with both the insurance and the annuity providers.

Safe Deposit Box

If your spouse had a safe deposit box, you will need to be listed as a signer on the account in order to open it. This would have needed to be done beforehand and most banks require this even if your spouse has passed. However, it is also possible to receive an order from the probate court so that you can have access to the box.

Talk to your Accountant

You should talk to your accountant as soon as possible because there are some taxes that may be required to be paid soon. For example, the estate tax is required to be paid within 9 months of the death. You may also need to file a separate tax return depending on the size of the estate.

Pay Outstanding Bills

If there is an estate, you will need to open an estate account or a trust account if necessary. There may be some bills that need to be paid, such as funeral expenses, utility bills, cred cards, etc. You should make sure that everything is kept up to date so that you will not have an issue when it comes time to handle the taxes for the year.

Post Office

You may need to talk to the post office if there are certain subscriptions or other items related to your spouse that needs to be canceled.

Set Up your own Checking Account

Eventually, you will want to set up your own checking account. Most banks will require a death certificate in order to remove your spouse from your account. It is usually also possible to simply close the account with your spouse on it and open a new one. However, the removal of your spouse is not required and you should wait a while to do so. It is actually advisable to leave your spouse on your account until you are certain that everything has come through that will have their name on it. Most banks will not allow you to deposit or cash checks against accounts without the person's name on them, so if you remove your spouse's name prematurely, you may find it difficult to handle life insurance payments or 401k deposits that need to be made. As a general rule of thumb, you should leave your spouse on your account for about a year, although some never remove them at all.

Chapter 4 - The Days After

Following the funeral, you may find yourself in a strange situation. While many people are around during and immediately following your funeral, people will begin to move on with their lives quickly and will soon forget about the situation that you are still living on a daily basis. It is common to find yourself in a place where you do not know what to do next. You may find that you are struggling to get through one day to the next and need some way to move on with your life, but don't even know how to begin to pick up the pieces.

These days and weeks, after everything has supposedly gone back to normal can be some of the toughest for you to experience. However, there are some things that you can do to help get you back on track and help you continue with the healing process.

Join a Support Group

There is no one better to understand what you are going through than people who are going through the same thing. If you have a friend who has also lost a spouse, you may find that you gravitate towards each other for comfort. If not, a support or bereavement group can be very comforting during this time. Here, you will be able to talk about what you are going through and gain comfort and support from others. You may also feel that you feel somewhat relieved to offer support and comfort to others in your same situation as well.

Write a Message to Your Spouse

Most often the death of a spouse is sudden and we are never left with the time that we need to say everything that we need to say. Sometimes, it may help to write a letter in order to express all the things that you did not get to say. After you write the letter, there are numerous ways that you can use the letter to help you move on. You can have the letter buried with your spouse if you have written it before the funeral, or you may simply prefer to read it aloud at their graveside. Or, you may want to keep it in order to reflect on your feelings at a later time. Regardless of what you do with the letter, you are likely to find some peace after you have written down what you would have wanted your last conversation to be with your spouse.

Have a Friend Stay with You

It may be difficult to be alone for quite a while after the funeral. Having a friend stay with you for a few weeks may be extremely helpful. You may see about staying with family during this time or with a friend yourself. More than likely, you will have people close to you that will be more than willing to help you out and help comfort you during this time. Although you may want to deal with this in private, this may also be a good time to begin the process of going through some of your spouse's belongings as well.

Try to Keep Your Normal Routine

Keeping your regular routine may help you move on more quickly. You should avoid getting into a rut where you avoid doing the things that you would normally be doing. It is easy to avoid getting out of bed in the morning or watching endless hours of TV in order to escape. However, this could lead you down a path towards clinical depression. It is important that you keep up your daily routine and return to it as quickly as possible following the loss of your spouse. If will be hard at first, but this will be the first step that you can take to help you get back to the healing process.

Reminisce

There is nothing wrong with remembering your spouse and trying to keep their memory alive. While they would want you to move on, your spouse would also want you to remember them as well. Take some time to go through all the old photos and videos of the memories that you made throughout your life together. This will be a difficult step to do and you may feel as though you need to put it off. There is also nothing wrong with this and you should only begin this step when you feel as if you are ready to do so. It is a good idea to start out slowly to make sure you are ready to handle it before you dive in too quickly.

The first few days will be hard, but eventually you will find yourself slipping back into the same routine that you had before you lost your spouse. However, you are likely to find that there is a piece of it that feels different than before. These feelings are completely normal and you should rely on the comfort of those around you to help get you through this tough time.

Chapter 5 - Picking Up the Pieces

Moving past the time that you are allowed off from work and returning to a normal time can be extremely difficult. While the world continues to spin, you are most likely feeling as if yours has stopped. You may find that it is difficult to return to an everyday mundane life, such as going to work and paying bills. However, these are the things that you must do in order to begin the process of healing and feeling normal once more.

It will be difficult to come home to an empty house with no one to greet you and no one to sit across from you at the dinner table. The silence may be so loud and you may find it difficult to realize that you are now truly alone.

You have created many memories together and have likely spent several years together and having that sense of balance removed in an instant is devastating. However, there are some things that you can do to help you get through these times and move on into the future.

The first thing that you should do is to complete any

request that your spouse asked before they passed away. If there were no last requests, consider finding something that you can do to honor their memory, such as make a donation in their name or have something dedicated in their name that will help serve others around you. This may help give you a sense of closure and help you move on.

You should also realize that it is going to take some time before you begin to feel somewhat normal again. This will not happen overnight and you will need to be patient as you go through the different stages that grief will take you through. Remember that grief is a journey and the length of time that it takes for you to complete it varies from person to person.

Although there are certain steps of grief that everyone will go through, it is not likely that you will experience them all in a certain order. You may find that you slip from one to the other repeatedly over the course of your recovery period. These are all natural feelings and you should embrace the feelings that you are having. You should never try to cover up or hide your feelings; this is the process that you must go through in order to heal and move on with your life.

There are always going to be those people who have

a preconceived notion about the proper way to grieve. You should ignore these people and if possible keep them out of your life, at least for a little while. Everyone experiences grief in a different manner and you are likely to come across people who think you are recovering too quickly and those who believe that you are not recovering quickly enough. However, if you do feel as if you are struggling to cope with the loss of your spouse, you should talk to a professional counselor about your situation. They will help to assess your emotions and help you realize whether they are normal or if you are experiencing extreme depression that needs to be dealt with.

Try to do something for yourself while you are healing. If you have always had a trip that you have wanted to take or something that you want to purchase, doing so may help you move towards healing a little bit faster. Try your best to be happy and look to fulfill your dreams and goals. Sometimes it helps to meet new people and find a new and exciting life that is different from the life you had before. You are likely to never be the same again and finding something new and fun to do can help fill the void that was left behind after your spouse's death.

Realize that change and happiness may not come

quickly or easily. You should always be patient with yourself and give yourself the time that you need to heal properly. Losing a spouse is one of the most difficult things to go through and recovering from such a loss will take a tremendous amount of time.

If you are having trouble coming home to an empty home, you may find comfort by adopting a pet. This will give you something to great you when you get home and may return purpose to your life. If you don't feel up to caring for an animal, it may be a good idea to adopt a cat because they require less maintenance than other animals. They clean themselves and do not need a lot of attention, but are willing to return your love and affection. Cats can be great to keep you company and will even lie in your lap when you want them to. Dogs are also a great option and will be excited to see you when you come home. Regardless of the pet that you choose, you should keep in mind that they will never replace your spouse. However, they may help fill some of the sorrow that you are feeling and help you to find some purpose and comfort in life once more. They can make you smile and will listen to every word that you say. Pets are very intuitive and will understand when you are upset. This may even give you a shoulder to cry on when you need one.

You may also find that keeping busy by volunteering your free time will help you feel somewhat better. Helping others is a great way to begin the healing process. There are also many hobbies that you can take on; visit the library and spend some time reading there…watch some movies or catch up on that TV series that you have always been interested in. You can also write letters to friends or visit people in the hospital or nursing homes to keep them company.

Chapter 6 - The Holidays

Just when you feel as if you are on the mend, a holiday will come up and throw you back into the stages of grief once more. The first few holidays, especially those like Christmas that are meant to spend with family, are extremely stressful and sad. Many say that they wish they could simply sleep through them so they don't have to go through the pain. The first few holiday seasons were exceptionally hard for me and my children. This is to be expected, and you shouldn't do more that you emotionally feel that you and your family can handle.

Another issue that you may find going into the holidays is all the memories that they bring up for you. You have likely made many throughout the years with your spouse and may find it difficult to cope when you are thinking about these memories. However, you may be able to actually use these memories to help you cope. Remember the happy times that you spent together and use them to keep the memory of your spouse alive.

Below are some things that you can do to help you cope with the holiday season:

Think ahead

As the holidays approach, think ahead and be prepared for the way that you will feel on each holiday as it approaches. This may help you anticipate and prepare for these holidays in advance.

Avoid staying alone all day

While you may feel tempted to spend the time by yourself, you should at least try and spend some time with family or friends throughout the day as well. It is never healthy to hide from the holiday and you will probably want and need some support from others while you try and get through this difficult time.

Don't expect to be your same happy self

While holidays are meant to bring happiness, don't feel that you should try and be your happy self throughout the season. You should expect to feel some sadness from time to time and it is completely natural to feel this way.

Give yourself some time to grieve

You should never try to bottle up your emotions while you are grieving. Sometimes giving yourself a specified time to grieve can help make the rest of the holiday more enjoyable or at least tolerable.

Change up your routine

Don't try to recreate the same holidays that you have had in the past. Mix it up a bit and try some new traditions. You don't have to change everything that you do during the holidays, just try one thing that is new for a change. Sing some carols with some friends or volunteer at a soup kitchen. Something that makes you feel useful can make a huge difference.

Warn your host and hostess

If you typically attend a certain party each year, be sure to call ahead and let them know that you may be leaving early. More than likely, they will understand and will not pressure you to stay longer than you are comfortable with doing so.

Wait 30 minutes

When you do arrive at the party, wait at least 30 minutes before leaving. This will give you time to adjust to the absence of your spouse and may help give you the time you need to loosen up and begin to relax and enjoy yourself. Don't be afraid to enjoy yourself either. This will also help with the healing process.

Take your own car

It is probably wise to drive yourself to the party or to ride with a friend who is willing to leave early if you need to. While you may feel completely fine to begin with, you may eventually tire of the party and feel as if you need to escape in order to deal with your grief.

Take a walk

If you do find yourself struggling to cope before the first 30 minutes, try going for a walk or retreating to the bathroom for a few minutes. This may help you to regain your composure and help you enjoy the party more.

Volunteer your time

In the end, if you do want to avoid the normal scene that you and your spouse are used to, try volunteering at a soup kitchen or visiting a shut-in instead. You may also want to pamper yourself during this time as well and take a trip to the spa or have a fun evening to yourself watching a movie.

Although it may be difficult, you will be able to get through the holidays. That's not to say that you won't be sad when they do come around again, but you should take comfort in the fact that you will be able to conquer them and move past them eventually.

Chapter 7 - Staying Strong for the Kids

When you lose a spouse, it may feel as if you cannot go on any longer. However, for those with children, it is very important that you do so. You kids need to know that they have you to turn to for support as they go through their own grieving process. Helping them go through the process of grieving may actually help you as well. As you are teaching your kids about the steps of grieving and helping them through the different phases that they are going through, you will begin to feel your own grief subside too.

It is a good idea that you have a close friend or family member offer support as well. If possible have this person stay with your family for a few days or weeks until you begin adjusting to life without the person who you have lost. This will give the kids someone to talk to if you are not available and will help give you some time to yourself when you need to grieve too. However, you should avoid sending your kids to another home while you are dealing with the grief. By doing so, you kids may begin to feel as if they have no one to turn to and that you cannot help them with their grief. When possible, it is best to attempt to grieve together as a family.

When you are trying to stay strong for your kids, there are some things that you can do to help all of you deal with your emotions at a better capacity. For example, you should talk to each other regularly. Talk about the person who has been lost and don't be afraid to let your children display emotions of anger and fear. Explain to them that you are also having these same feelings and that they are a natural part of the grieving process. If you are struggling to find the right words to say to your kids, you may want to talk to a counselor for a bit of advice.

It may also help that you visit a family counselor to help you all get back on the road to recovery. Sometimes a professional is just the person that a family needs after a loss as significant as a spouse and a parent have died.

While you are going through these phases, just make sure that you keep in mind that it is important for you to stay strong for your kids. They need some strong structure to help get them through the days ahead in order to help them get through this difficult time and have a productive life in the future.

Chapter 8 - Consoling the Kids

If you have kids, you will need to remember that they are also grieving as well. While it may be difficult to process, there are ways that you can help your kids get through the grieving process easier.

Things to remember:

- Many kids will want to tell their story after a parent has died.

- Telling their story is one way that they deal with the loss and grieving process.

- Adults can help children by listening to their stories.

  They should also continue their normal daily routines, receive extra care and will want to feel connected, both to the remaining parent and the one that has passed away as well.

What do children need when they lose a parent?
First of all, they will want and need to tell their story. Don't be surprised if they begin sharing what

happened along with where they were and when they learned about the death of their parent. They may also begin sharing what it was like for them hearing about this heath. Just remember that this is all part of their healing process. Adults should listen to these children to help them deal with the grieving process.

Continuing their normal routine is also very important. They should return to school and remain active in the same activities that they took part in before the loss. Everywhere possible, it is important that they remain as comfortably in their routine as normal. You should also talk to your child's school so that they will be there to help your child if they need to speak with the counselor.

You should also make certain that you are providing your kids with a lot of extra care throughout their day. Give them extra hugs and make sure that they do not begin to feel lonely. Kids and adults alike will go through many of the same stages of grief. It is also a good idea to ask a family member to come to your home to help take care of your child during the first few weeks following the death. This may help when your own grief is at its highest. However, you should be careful about separating yourself from your kids during this time. Keep them close whenever possible. When a family loses a member of the family, especially one like a parent or a spouse, it is natural for the family to feel incomplete. It may feel natural to withdraw from one another for a bit, but this is the time that children may begin to feel lonely and disconnected from their remaining parent.

Following the death of a parent, children need to feel closer to their remaining parent rather than be pushed away from them. This will help both of you cope with the loss that you are feeling. I arranged special times with each daughter individually, where it was just the two of us, one on one, for the day. We would go out to breakfast, get manicures, or shop for a special toy. During that time we could talk about what they were thinking about and if anything was bothering them, we could discuss it. I wanted them to still feel special, and not pushed aside because of my grief.

Below are some very specific ways that you can help your children cope and begin to heal during this time:

- Addressing their fears and anxieties

- Reassuring them that they are not the ones to blame

- Listening to them carefully

- Answering their questions about death

- Understanding and accepting that they have feelings of grief as well

- Help them feel safe

- Respect them and their personal way of coping

- Help them deal with the emotions

- Involve them with the things that are going on

- Reminisce with them about the parent who passed

More than likely there are some very specific questions that you child may be asking themselves. Although they may not ask you these questions directly, you should try and answer them for them:

- Who will take care of me now?

- Am I going to get sick?

- Is it my fault?

Children rely on their parents to feel safe and with the death of one, this can change the way a child looks at the world around them. Make sure that you are giving your child encouragement and reassuring that it is ok to feel safe. Many children may even have fears that they will become sick and dye as well, so it may be a good idea to visit the doctor for a simple check-up. Before you attend the appointment, however, you should have a conversation with your doctor so that they are prepared for the types of questions that your child may be ready to ask them.

Communication

It is probably the hardest thing to keep an open communication with children after you have lost your spouse. Some children may not require communication, but will need a way to express their feelings.

Below are some of the ways to can help them to express theirs:

- When you talk about the deceased parent, use their name

- Help them create a container that holds memories that they feel are special about the parent who has passed

- Make copies of photos for your children

- Make a photo album or a collection of stories about the parent who has passed

- Write down memories in a journal

Answer a set of questions about the parent who has passed, such as:

- Where did they enjoy going the most?

- What did they enjoy watching on TV?

- What was their favorite meal or dessert?

-

Give your child a special item that belonged to their deceased parent. This might be a special piece of clothing, a piece of jewelry, or any other object that is significant.

Make sure that you devote time to listen to your kids. Unlike adults, kids will not be ready to openly talk about what is going on except in small bursts of conversations. You should make sure that you are offering your ear several times throughout the day.

Make new memories together.

What about therapy?
There are times when children try to hide their grief from their remaining parent as a way to protect them. Because of this, there are certain times when the children may need professional help to help them cope with their loss. It may be difficult to see the signs that a child needs professional help because they are masked along with the other signs of a grieving child.

If you notice that you child is undergoing the following symptoms, you should consider finding professional help for them:

- Continuing to have difficulties when talking about what has happened and the parent that they have lost

- Showing anger and aggression

- Having physical issues: stomach aches, headaches

- Difficulty sleeping

- If their eating patterns have been disrupted, either they are eating too little or they are eating too much

- Withdrawing from their friends and those who are about them.

- Difficult in school: Getting bad grades, behaving poorly, having a hard time concentrating, etc

- Continued issues with guilt and blame

- Becoming self-destructive and talking about hurting themselves
-

Therapy can be quite beneficial to a child who is older, because it will give them the space they need to talk about what is going on, in an environment that is safe and nonjudgmental. There may be times when the therapist wants you to come in to talk together with your kids. This may help all of you heal easier.

Play therapy is often used for children who are around the age of eight. Keep in mind that even small children and infants are affected when they lose a parent. They may not be able to manage their feelings as well and these issues may not be as obvious as with older kids. You should take time to help them cope as well.

When choosing a family counselor, make sure that the one that you are considering has experience dealing with kids who have lost parents at the age your children are at now.

Chapter 9 - Coping with Tragedy

There are times when tragedy has taken a spouse away, such as a natural disaster or some other sudden event like a car accident. There may also be times when there are many others who are dealing with the same grief and tragedy situation that you are going through yourself. It is natural to feel a sense of anxiety and stress during this time, especially if the media is involved and you are continuing to live out the tragedy when you watch the news or step outside your home.

When facing a tragedy, you are most likely facing some of the following emotions that are common immediately following a tragedy:

• Shock

• Fear

• Disorientation

• Numbness

• Nightmares

- Anger

- Depression

- Feeling powerless

- Issues with your diet

- Crying excessively

- Physical pain

- Having a hard time sleeping

When you are feeling these issues, there are also ways that you can help yourself cope and get through the difficult time. For starters, you should talk about what you are going through with others. This can help relieve some of the stress that you are feeling and help you connect with others who are going through the same thing and feelings that you are.

You should also make it a point to spend time with your family and friends. Being around people who love you may help to get you through the tough times ahead. If you cannot be with them physically, talk to them regularly on the phone. You should also encourage your children to talk to you about their feelings.

Make sure you take care of yourself. While it is natural to stop caring about yourself during this time, you should make sure that you are resting, eating right and exercising. Grief can add a lot of stress to your life and by taking care of yourself, you will be able to eliminate some of it.

Don't overdo it. Remember that grieving is a process, you should not try to do more than small tasks at once. While it is good to stay busy, you should try to stick with one thing at a time before moving on to something else.

Often times, a tragedy brings about a need for assistance. If you can help, you should try to help as much as possible. For example, you can give blood or try and help others who have lost loved ones. If there has been structural damage to your town, see what you can do to help to rebuild it. Helping with the rebuilding efforts can provide you with a sense of purpose and help you to have structure in your life again.

You should avoid drinking alcohol and taking drugs. It is important that you embrace the feelings that you are having rather than try to cover them up. This will help you to heal faster. When you rely on drugs and alcohol to numb the pain, you are only prolonging your grief and making it more difficult to move on past the situation that you are in.

Make sure that you ask for help when you need it. You should still be able to function on a daily basis and if you find yourself struggling, make sure that you talk to someone about it. Whether it is a close family friend or a professional counselor, you should never be afraid to ask for help when you need it.

Keep in mind that your children are also struggling to grieve and you will need to help them deal with the effects of the tragedy as well. Make sure that you talk to your kids about what happened and help them to move on past this tragedy and into their future.

Chapter 10 - Suicide

Losing a spouse is difficult, but when you lose yours to suicide, there are many feelings that can be added in addition to the ones that are already common with grief. Along with the typical feelings that one experiences with grief; shock, anger, guilt, despair; you will also be adding the idea that there are people out there who will blame you for the death.

You may think that you should have known or wonder if it was your fault. These feelings are completely natural, but you need healthy ways to deal with these items. Below are some things to consider and do when you are dealing with the suicide of your spouse.

First, you should try and keep in touch with your loved ones and friends. They will be able to offer comfort and understanding during this time. Make sure that the people who are in your life will listen to you when you need them and will provide you with the shoulder you need to lean upon and cry upon, as needed. Avoid relying on those people who have expressed feelings of blame towards you or ill thoughts towards your spouse. Now is not the time to be dealing with these types of people.

Don't be afraid to grieve how you want to grieve. With a suicide, you are likely to be under more scrutiny than you would normally be under with a typical death of a spouse. However, you need to continue to grieve in the way that works for you and don't be afraid of what others will say or think about the process you are going through. The important thing is that you are healing and moving on with your life.

Keep in mind that you will have painful memories that surface from time to time. When a spouse commits suicide, it is often their spouse who finds them after they have passed. Seeing your loved one in this manner can bring back extremely shocking and disturbing images into your mind from time to time. Due to the sensitivity of your spouse's death, it may be a good idea to avoid certain family traditions because they will bring back those memories. Try not to rush your recovery process. You should realize that it is going to take some time before you begin to feel normal again. Allow the healing to occur at its own pace.

You may also want to join a support group for others who have been affected by suicide. While losing a spouse is a difficult thing to handle, losing them to a suicide can be even more difficult and it may take others who have been through the same

situation to help you heal from the tragedy
.

While you are dealing with the painful loss of your spouse, try and remember the following points:

- Your spouse did not want to hurt you, but they did not feel as if they could go on through the situation they were feeling having to deal with any longer.

- You should talk to others about your spouse and draw strength from their happy memories. You will feel a number of emotions and it will help if you are able to talk about them with those who knew and loved your spouse.

- It is alright to cry and you will do this often just as you would if your spouse has died from natural causes.

- Remember the happy times that you shared together.

- Avoid thinking about the way your spouse died and don't dwell on the thought of their suicide. This will only bring tremendous pain and a sense of not understanding what has happened.

Above all, you need to grieve. People whose spouses have committed suicide tend to forget that it is alright for them to grieve. They may even have those around them who look down on them for their grief and begin saying negative things about the family or their deceased spouse. You should avoid these people and grieve just as you would with a normal death.

Chapter 11 - Anger

After your spouse dies, it is natural to feel some anger; anger at your spouse for abandoning you, anger at God for taking your spouse, anger at the circumstance; you may even begin to feel anger towards yourself for being angry. However, anger is also a normal and natural part of the grieving process. It is also something that is not discussed as regularly as other feelings that you are having following the death of your spouse. Unfortunately, anger will not go away just because we ignore it.

Most often, you will begin to feel guilty over your anger and wonder if your feelings are normal. It is difficult to find the proper way to express these feelings of anger and we typically end up with one of two outcomes. Either we scream out loud or we cry excessively. Neither of these items help us to deal with the anger that we are feeling.

You should realize that anger comes in many forms. There may even be physical ailments that come along with it, such as headaches and muscle fatigue and pain. You may find that you are irritable over the smallest things or that you are resorting to strange habits, like excessive shopping or throwing out all of your spouse's possessions; anything that is excessively different from what you would normally do.

You may also feel as if no one knows and understands exactly what you are going through. Most of the time the surviving spouse will become overwhelmed with advice from others who have not experienced the pain of losing a spouse, or worse, they avoid the surviving spouse altogether because they do not know what to say. This can leave the surviving spouse with a sense of loneliness and when you combine loneliness with anger, you can easily become miserable. If you do find yourself in an extremely low position, it is best to talk with a professional counselor who can help you deal with your emotions in a more positive manner. Although your feelings are normal, you may be able to transition into the next stage of grief faster with the aid of a counselor.

One of the best ways that you can deal with the anger of losing your spouse is to write down the feelings that you are having. It may help to actually write your spouse a letter and tell them exactly how you feel. Don't hold back and let all of your emotions out onto the paper. Continue writing until you have said everything that needs to be said. Deep down, you know that your spouse never intended to leave you. However, our deaths are not in our control and their time had been completed here on earth. Although you may be angry that you did not get more time with your spouse and that you weren't able to say goodbye, you can take a moment to write out your final thoughts in a letter. This can be especially helpful if you have had a disagreement or were at odds when your spouse passed. Writing a letter to your spouse will help you to spell out the feelings of regret and anger that you did not have the opportunity to have the matter resolved.

The most important thing, is to let the anger go once you have completed the letter. You can do whatever you want to with it, bury it with, burn it, tear it into little pieces, whatever you need to do to let the anger go and move on with your life. Anger does not serve you, so let it go and start living your life without that heavy burden. Your spouse would want you to be happy.

Chapter 12 - Regret and Guilt

Losing a spouse can bring about great feelings of regret and guilt. Regrets could be in regards to all the things that you had wanted to do with your spouse and never got around to, like taking certain vacations. You may also feel regret when you think about their death and thinking that you should have been with them, or died alongside them.

Guilt can also come in many forms; guilt for still being alive, guilt for not being able to save them; guilt for an argument that you had had the day that they passed, or a number of other reasons. The important thing to remember is that these feelings of guilt and regret are completely natural. You are simply going through a portion of the healing process. You should keep in mind that their death was not your fault and there is nothing that you could have done differently to have changed the outcome. Although, deep down, you know that this is true, it may still be difficult to deal with the feelings that come along with their death.

Causes of Regret and Guilt
Research   has   shown   that   people   tend   to

overestimate their control over certain things in their lives. Following the loss of a spouse, survivors will frequently begin thinking about all the "could have" and "should have" items that they could have done to save their loved one. It is common to wonder why your spouse died, but you were left to live. This is especially common for couples who were involved in a car accident and one spouse died, but the other survived and can be even more so if the surviving spouse was at fault for causing the accident.

Types of Feelings

When you begin looking at feelings of guilt there are three different types of survivor's guilt; general, parental, with specific incident. In most instances, the guilt that you are feeling is general guilt. This is the most common and covers most circumstances of guilt following the death of a loved one.

Parents will feel parental guilt after they lose a child, which is unique to parents losing a child. When there is something specific that caused the person to pass, such as an accident or suicide, there is another type of guilt associated with the passing called with specific incident. All three types of guilt are unique and bring about some different types of feelings to the one who has lost their loved one.

Effects of Guilt and Regret

Self-blame and doubt are two of the most common feelings that are felt after the death of a loved one and can trigger anxiety and increased suffering. Those who are experiencing survivor guilt may find that their lives are impacted in many different ways and can affect your ability to be productive, cope with your grief and have a positive outlook on life.

Coping Strategies

If you are dealing with guilt there are many things that you can do to help deal with these feelings and move on past your grief and loss. The most important thing is to build up a support system that is made up of close friends and family that you can confide in. You also need to take care of your health and nutrition. Exercise regularly and getting a good night's sleep is also important when trying to cope with feelings of guilt and regret after the loss of a spouse.

Finding Help

If you do find that you are struggling to deal with the guilt that you are feeling, you may find that receiving professional help is necessary. When the feelings of guilt that you are experience do not subside over time and you begin to feel depressed due to your guilt, you should talk to your doctor. There are many support groups and other resources that you can rely on when you are trying to deal with your feelings of guilt. Keep in mind that these feelings are completely normal, but by receiving help from a professional, you may be able to move on more easily.

Chapter 13 - The Healing Power of Time

One thing that is often said when dealing with grief is that time heals all wounds. While it is true that your pain will subside over time and you will begin to function normally again, feeling completely whole and normal does not often occur. There are times, even years in the future, when you will feel sadness over the loss of your spouse. Even after you have moved on you may find yourself in a sudden state of sadness over your loss. Maybe there is a memory that sparks the return of your sadness and loss or perhaps you have simply gone through another year without them. Keep in mind that these continued feelings of sadness are completely natural. You have lost the person that you had intended to spend the rest of your life with and while they spent the rest of their lives with you, you have been robbed of your time with them.

You are never going to forget your spouse, and you shouldn't try. Instead, when a memory threatens to overtake your happiness, try to focus on the memory of the good time instead. If you are walking through a store and smell the cologne or perfume that your spouse used to wear and are immediately rushed with an overwhelming sense of sadness, take a deep breath and a moment to remember the one that you loved.

Realize that grief is a process and is never completely healed entirely. These feelings are natural and you may still expect to see your spouse walk through the door to your home or expect to pick up the phone and hear their voice once more. Although this will not be possible, you will eventually begin to return to a normal functioning life and even though you may be happy, it doesn't mean that you miss your deceased spouse any less than you did the day they passed.

Dealing with the pain of losing a spouse is one of the hardest things that you will ever have to do. For some it is the hardest thing to deal with. However, with time, you will begin to see a positive change in your life and may even find that you are ready to share your love with someone else. You should never feel guilty about wanting to move on after your spouse has passed. Instead, embrace your memories and realize that your spouse would want you to be happy and move on with your life.

However, if you find that you are unable to function in everyday life, you should seek help from a professional. While there is a natural grieving process that everyone must go through, there are circumstances where someone is not able to deal with the grief and pain in a manner that is healthy. If you find yourself in this situation, you will need to seek professional help. This is extremely important if you are suffering from an addiction or are thinking of committing suicide or causing harm to yourself because of your loss and your grief. The bottom line is, if you feel are not able to make steps to move forward with your life, you should seek guidance from a professional.

Chapter 14 - Going Through Belongings

After you lose a spouse, it may be difficult to return to your normal life. While some people feel as if they should leave everything the same, others may feel as if they want to rid their lives of every possession that their spouse ever had. Both situations can be harmful if taken to the extreme. It is expected to keep some mementos of your spouse; however, you should never keep everything as it was before they passed. You will need to go through their things and remove unneeded items that you will no longer need. This may be a bit of a process that takes several months to complete. However, you will find that it helps with your grieving process.

Take some time to allow other loved ones of your spouse to choose some items that they wish to keep for themselves. For example, if you have a daughter, she may want to hang onto some personal belongs like jewelry or a wedding dress that belonged to her mother. It is important to give your kids the opportunity that they need in order to grieve with you as well.

You should also avoid getting rid of everything prematurely. Take the time that you need to process the situation to the fullest measure. If you do feel that it is necessary to remove all the items that belonged to your spouse from your home, it is probably a good idea to rent a storage unit and have the items stored until you are ready to go through them yourself.

There are multiple ways that you can handle removing your loved ones items from your home and the method which you choose is entirely up to you. Some people may try and force you into allowing them to help you with the process in order to prevent you from being alone with your pain. However, it is important to realize that everyone grieves differently and you may need this time to reflect on your pain alone. However, if you do feel as though you need help going through the items, don't be afraid to ask for it. There will be people around you who will be more than willing to help you sort through the items and will give you the shoulder that you need to cry on when the time comes.

Another thing to keep in mind is that if the pair of you has small children, there may be some items that you will want to keep for the kids that they can have as they get older. You should keep them in mind as well and choose meaningful things that they can treasure that belonged to their parent. Be sure to keep these keepsakes in a safe location until they are old enough to care for them properly. It may be a good idea to let them have a couple of items now that they can keep and also save some of the items that are more special than others until they are older.

It took me six months to even begin to go through my husband's clothing. I kept most of his t-shirts and had them sewn into quilts for my children. I also had a few of his flannel shirts sewn into pillows and teddy bears for me and my girls. This was a comforting way to hold on to his things, but still put them to a resourceful use, instead of taking up room in the closet. My kids can snuggle up with their blankets and teddy bears and feel close to their father. If your children are grown, you may want to allow them to pick out some items that they would like to keep or allow them to help you go through the items that are in the home. This will be a great way to help your family heal and move on with your lives and may offer you some closure are well.

Keep in mind that removing the items that belonged to your spouse will be difficult and it may take some time before you are ready to do so. If you find that you are unable to let go of items, you may want to see a counselor or talk to a support group who can help you to let go and move on.

Chapter 15 - Letting Go

When you lose your spouse, there will come a time when it is necessary to let them go. However, hard this may be it will be something you have to go through at some point or another. This is, perhaps, one of the hardest things about losing a spouse; to deal accepting the fact that you are never going to see your loved one again. Keep in mind that this is one of the last steps that you will experience when you are dealing with the loss of your spouse, and it will take some time to get to that point. The amount of time that it takes for a person to reach that milestone varies from one individual to the next, but most everyone goes through the same stages.

You should get to this place in your grief journey on your own, and never feel pressured or rushed by others to get there sooner than you have to. However, you will have many people who will give you advice that will encourage you to rush on through with the process and move on quickly. While this works with some people, it does not with everyone. While some feel the need to move on quickly, others would rather embrace the pain that they are feeling and allow the process to take a longer period of time. Whatever way the process works best for you, is how you should deal with letting go.

Make sure that you give yourself a proper amount of time to go through the grieving process, regardless of the amount of time that it takes you to get there. It is a good idea to build a support group that can help you get through this difficult time to the point where you are ready to let go. Keep in mind that you should never allow them to pressure the way that you grieve. By altering your grieving pattern in order to please those around you, you are not being given the chance to grieve properly and may find that you are in a worse position further down the road than you would have been in the first place.

You must avoid participating in certain things that can be harmful. Some people begin relying on drugs and alcohol or dangerous activities to help them let go of the person that they loved. This is only masking your pain and you should seek guidance if you find yourself in this position.

One of the first steps in letting go of the one that you loved and lost is forgiving yourself. Most often, people who lose a spouse or a close loved one tend to blame themselves for the outcome of their death. It is important that you realize there was nothing that you could have done that would have changed the outcome. Before you can move on and let go of your spouse for good, you will need to start with this very important step.

Chapter 16 - Dealing with Depression

Depression is a normal part of dealing with the pain of losing your spouse. However, if you begin to feel that you are struggling to move on or are considering suicide, you should seek professional help immediately. There are many hotlines and support groups available that can help you with the process of dealing with the loss of your spouse and the feelings of depression that you are feeling. They can be very helpful during this time. Keep in mind that losing a spouse affects every portion of your life; mentally, emotionally and physically. There is likely little that you can do that will not remind you of the one that you have lost and you are likely to think of them on a daily basis, at least at first.

While symptoms of depression are often the same ones that you would generate after losing a spouse, you may be experiencing severe depression and need professional guidance. In fact, it is estimated that nearly half of people who lose a spouse experience severe depression during the first month following their passing. With this common statistic, it may be comforting to realize that you are not alone in your feelings and that many others have gone through the same process that you are now going through yourself. This is why support groups can be so helpful. You can connect with others just like you and learn things that have helped others get through the pain.

One important thing that you should keep in mind while attending support groups, is that you should never compare someone else's experience and pain with your own. Everyone is their own individual and react to pain and grief in various different ways. You should try not to be judgmental and look at other's pain as a sign of weakness because you would not want them to do the same to you. While you are in the support group to gain support from the others involved, you need to remember that you are also there to offer support to them as well. It may be a good idea to pair up with someone that you feel especially close to and rely on each other to help you get through this difficult time.

When you pick a partner from your support group, it is important that you avoid forming an intimate relationship with a member of the opposite sex. With the emotions that you both are experiencing, it would be easy to fall into a relationship with someone who already knows the pain that you are going through. These relationships are usually never healthy and can cause deeper feelings of regret and guilt further down the road. It may also cause you to have the need to cut ties with the other members of your support group if the relationship goes badly. This could also set you further back in the process of completing the stages of grief and truly moving on with your life in a healthy manner.

Chapter 17 - Ask for Help

One of the most common things that people tell someone who has just lost a close loved one like a spouse is, "Let me know if you need anything." While this is a fantastic thing to say, it is another thing to actually mean it. You will probably have some very close friends and family that you can rely on heavily during this time who will help you move on and get through some of the tough times that are in front of you. Many people will bring dinner and offer to do things for you and you are likely to accept it happily.

However, there are times when there is something that you need specifically. You should never be afraid to call those people who have offered their assistance when you need help. Most often, these people will be more than happy to help you get through a tough moment, whether it be running to the grocery store when you don't feel up to it or handling chores that you would normally do with your spouse. It is also understandable to want to do some things on your own, so you should never feel as if you are forced to allow people to help you out with certain things. You do need to be polite and grateful for everything that you friends and family do for you, though.

If you are ready to have some time alone, gently tell them what you are looking for and they will be more than happy to oblige. Likewise, when you do need their help call and ask nicely if they would mind helping you out for a while. People tend to be very understanding when you are going through a tough time and many will be more than happy to help you in any way that they can. After you have gotten through the difficult spell, you should remember to thank those who helped you in your hour of need. While no thanks will be necessary, it will let the person know that you appreciate the help that they offered and help you to keep a strong friend throughout the rest of your life.

I will be forever grateful to my best friend, who helped me when I was at my worst moment. I could always count on her to cry to and to give me strength when I was weak and weary. She helped me with my daughters, which made it easier for them to cope. If you have a strong friendship bond with someone, don't hesitate to reach out and ask them for help. Don't hesitate to call them when you need them. A true friend will be there for you, and now is the time you need it most.

When you lose a spouse, you need to have those around you who are going to help you to move on and grieve properly at the same time. By relying on those around you to help you out with simple tasks, you can give yourself the time that you need to grieve properly and remember your spouse. However, it is also necessary that you do not begin to take advantage of your friends while you are going through the healing process. Not only will this damage your friendships, it can actually lead you down a path of staying stuck in grief for a longer period of time than is necessary. You should only rely on your friends when you truly need them and never out of habit.

Also, make sure that you don't always call your friend when you are in need of something. Keeping a healthy relationship with others around you is important for the healing process and you should maintain a healthy relationship with them outside of their help for you. Share your feelings with them and always thank them for everything that they are doing to help you. Sometimes a friend that is willing to share a caring shoulder to cry on or an ear to listen makes all the difference in the world when you are looking to move past the loss of your spouse.

Chapter 18 - Discovering Secrets

Unfortunately, not every marriage was built on trust, and some spouses have learned secrets that their spouse was hiding after their death. Some have been simple secrets, like hiding away some money for a rainy day, but others were larger, more dangerous, such as an affair or even a child that you were unaware of. Learning these secrets after your spouse has passed can be excruciatingly painful and you will be left with many questions regarding why your spouse would have hidden these items from you. Not having answers to these questions can make you doubt the very core of your marriage and the life that was built around it. If you do find yourself in this extreme circumstance, you should also know that you are not alone. There are others out there who have gone through the same exact thing, although your circumstance will still vary from others with similar stories.

There are a few ways that you can handle learning about the secrets that your spouse was keeping from you and it is probably best to seek professional help when dealing with these issues. One way that is very helpful is to join a support group and look for others who are like yourself and have similar stories. Simply being able to talk about what you are going through may make a huge difference in the recovery process. You may also feel as though you should learn everything about the items that your spouse was keeping from you. While this may be a helpful way to get you through this process, you should probably talk to a counselor before you begin an obsessive hunt for something that you spouse had been keeping to them self.

Probably the hardest part of dealing with secrets that your spouse may have been keeping from you is, not knowing why the secrets were kept in the first place. It is normal to feel anger and betrayal towards your spouse and to question the very being of your relationship. Although there are bound to be secrets that are kept in every marriage, some are larger than others and have a bigger impact on your life once they have been found out. For some larger issues, you may need to consult with an attorney in order to determine how they need to be handled.

For example, if your spouse has another child that you are not aware of, you may need to find what you are required to do in regards to the estate in caring for the child after their parent has passed away. You may also find that this affects your life insurance policy as well as any settlement from retirement a pension funds as well. For these matters, it is best to seek guidance from both an attorney and your accountant.

Above all, you must be able to move past the secrets into a place where you are at peace with everything that has occurred. This will likely require guidance from a professional guidance counselor and quite a bit of time to deal with the issues that this betrayal has caused in your life.

Chapter 19 - Grief Journal or Letters

When you feel you are ready, writing to your loved one in a journal or in the form of a letter, will give you a sense of connection with them. You may want to start doing this right away, or it may take years before you can put your feelings into tangible words on paper. This healing exercise will help you work through any guilt or shame that may be unsettled with the deceased. You may not have been able to say goodbye to them, and by doing so in a letter, you are giving yourself the closure needed to continue living your own life.

You may just feel like talking to them, and telling them about the latest events going on in your life. Whatever you decide to write about is okay. Nobody else but you has to read it. It is also therapeutic to look back at your journal or letters in the future, to see how far you have come in your grief. Most of the time, once you start writing, the words will just flow, and you will end up feeling like a weight has been lifted.

Below are some prompts to get you started, if you feel like you are unsure what to write about:

- What are your feelings at this moment?

- Is there anything left unsaid that you need to get off of your chest?

- If you were not present when they passed away, express your last goodbye.

- How do you plan on keeping their memory alive?

- What are some memories of them that make you smile?

- Do you need to forgive them or ask for forgiveness?

- Are you regretful for anything you did or didn't do while they were alive?

- What do you miss most about them?

- Explain the depth of your love for them and the influence they had on your life.

- Write about the current events in your life and what has happened since they passed.

Chapter 20 - Keeping their Memory Alive

After you lose a spouse, you are most likely looking for a way to honor their memory and keep their memory alive in the people who knew them. There are a number of ways that you can accomplish this, each of which can be beneficial to moving on with your life and continuing the process of healing.

When you are looking for a way to keep your loved one's memory alive, consider the following ideas:

Make a donation

Making a donation to a charity that your spouse would have supported in their name is a great option. There are many to choose from so going through the process of finding the right one could take some time. You may want to explain to the charity that you are donating this in the name of your late spouse so that they can appreciate how special the gift is.

Start a Foundation

Start a foundation in the name of your spouse, and use the money to help other wives and children in a similar situation.

Hold an Annual Fundraiser

Start an annual fundraiser in memory of your loved one, to support a cause they were passionate about or for medical research for an illness they had.

Run a Marathon

This can be extremely helpful if your spouse died of a specific disease or cancer. Marathons are a great way to honor their memory and give you purpose and meaning. You will need to train extensively to be able to complete the marathon and you may end up finding a new hobby that you love.

Get your degree

If you never finished high school or college, now might be a good time to go back and finish up your education. While you may never do anything with the degree you obtain, working towards a goal that is in memory of your spouse will be extremely special and when you achieve it, you will feel even better about the journey that you have taken.

Pursue your dreams

Most everyone has a dream that they have put on the back burner throughout their life. By picking it back up and pursuing your dreams, you will be able to work towards something that you have always wanted to accomplish. You should realize that your spouse would have been very proud of you by going after what you desire the most and you should be very proud of yourself.

One of the best ways that you can honor the memory of your spouse is to move on with your life. While this may be difficult, you should know that this is what your spouse would have wanted and you should honor their wishes. However, it is also important that you give yourself the proper amount of time to heal and deal with your grief. The amount of time that this takes varies form one person to the next, so there is no set time limit involved. But, when you have healed, don't be afraid to move on with your life and live happy once more.

Chapter 21 - Dating Again

One of the most difficult portions of the moving on process after your spouse has passed away, is deciding if you are ready to move on and date again. While some never end up dating again, others begin dating rather quickly.

The proper amount of time really depends on the person involved. You may find that you are ready to move on right away, but your friends may feel as though you should wait longer. While the exact time frame is not that important, you do need to make sure that you truly are ready to begin dating before you begin the process over once more.

I did not start dating again until three years after my husband passed away. Luckily, I didn't have to date very long until a co-worker introduced me to my current husband. I was a little reserved at first, but it felt nice to finally have a connection with a man again. He was very patient with me, and we were married two years after we met. I am happy once again, but will never forget my first love and the moments we shared together. I like to think that he had a part in my finding my current husband. I know he would want me to be happy and well taken care of.

Some children will never be happy with their parents dating, and this is a conversation that you will need to have with them. I feel that by taking several years before dating again, gave my daughters time to adjust to our new life, without bringing in someone new. You may want to sit them down beforehand and inform them that you are going to be dating again so that they are prepared for the shock of seeing you with another person. Explain to them that you still love and miss the parent that has passed very much, but that you need to have a companion to help you be happy with your life. Older children will be able to understand this, but if you have younger kids, you may want to be a little vague.

One thing that is important when you are beginning to date again is to avoid getting into a relationship that is not healthy. If the relationship that you enter into is abusive or forms other types of negative energy like drug and alcohol abuse, you need to end the relationship and seek professional guidance immediately.

It is important that you avoid rushing into a serious relationship following the death of your spouse. You need to have the time necessary to grieve and heal, but some have found that moving on is a great step in the healing process.

Below are some simple questions that you can ask yourself to know if you are ready to start dating once more:

- Do you understand that you are not guilty of wanting to move on with your life?

- Do you feel like you have reclaimed yourself?

- Have you given up on the anger portion of the grief process?

- Can you leave your relationship in the past and not bring the remnants of it with you to your next relationship?

- Can you be happy by yourself?

- Are you able to go out by yourself and have fun with friends and family?

- Do you feel as though you are available emotionally?

- Do you feel capable of trusting someone again?

- Are you using silly fears or assumptions to

keep you off the dating market?

In the end, when you are ready to begin dating again, you will know that you are ready. Keep in mind that you have probably been out of the dating game for quite some time and it may be awkward at first. However, with a little practice and some patient from your date, you will easily be able to get the hang of it and begin the process of building new memories with someone else. While your spouse will never be replaced in your heart, it is possible to build a life with someone new that is just as great as it was with the spouse who you loved and lost.

Chapter 22 - Conclusion

Dealing with the death of a spouse is one of the hardest things that you can go through, even if you had been expecting their death. There is nothing quite like losing your life partner, and you may feel it difficult to move on and face the world again. Just remember that the feelings that you are having are most likely normal. You should embrace them and rely on others to help you get through the time. If you feel like screaming, scream…if you feel like crying, find a shoulder to cry on…and don't be afraid to ask for help when you need it.

If you are having a difficult time coping with the loss of your spouse, don't be afraid to talk to a specialist. While the feelings may be normal, you may still feel that it is best to seek professional guidance. This is a perfectly natural thing to do and may help you feel better in the end.

The most important thing to remember is that there is no right way to deal with the death of a spouse. However, if you take some proactive steps toward the recovery process, you may find that you feel at peace sooner and are able to move on with your life at a much faster pace than if you did nothing at all.

<u>Online Grief Support</u>

<u>Sisterhood of Widows</u>: Widow support.
http://sisterhoodofwidows.com

<u>Widow and Widower Support</u>:
http://www.nationalwidowers.org/support-groups/#.VDV2X_ldWDo

<u>Survivors of Suicide</u>:
http://www.survivorsofsuicide.com

<u>Alliance of Hope</u>: For suicide survivors.
http://www.allianceofhope.org

<u>Healing The Grief:</u> This book is featured on
http://healingthegrief.com
Articles, poems and links to helpful resources and
other books on the topic of grief and how to heal.

About the Author

Amanda Banks became a widow at a young age. Her goal is to take the tragic experience of losing her husband, and use it to help others in the same situation. Her first book, "Heartbreak to Healing" has been cathartic for her to write, as she revisits the path of grief, that she walked down years ago. Amanda lives in the USA with her two daughters and her second husband, who support her on her journey through loss and counseling others

<u>NOTES</u>

AMANDA BANKS

81463116R00058

Made in the USA
San Bernardino, CA
07 July 2018